A Guide for l

MW01283316

The Adventures of Tom Sawyer

in the Classroom

Based on the book written by Mark Twain

*This guide written by **Katie Eyles, M.Ed.***

Teacher Created Resources, Inc.
12621 Western Avenue
Garden Grove, CA 92841
www.teachercreated.com
ISBN: 978-1-57690-637-8
©2002 Teacher Created Resources, Inc.
Reprinted, 2019
Made in U.S.A.

Edited by
Stephanie Buehler, Psy.D.

Illustrated by
Bruce Hedges

Cover Art by
Kevin Barnes

Table of Contents

Introduction

While reading the pages of Mark Twain's *The Adventures of Tom Sawyer*, you can almost see the steamboats ambling up the mighty Mississippi, feel the soft river mud between your toes, and smell the chicken frying to a crispy brown. This classic novel transports the reader from a time filled with traffic, TVs, and computers to a simpler time filled with the adventures of a young boy named Tom.

The aim of this literature unit is to help the instructor make this classic tale a pleasant, entertaining, and educational experience. The following materials are included in this unit:

- Sample Lesson Plans

- Pre-reading Activities

- Biographical Sketch

- Chronological List of Works by Mark Twain

- Book Summary

- Vocabulary Lists and Suggestions

- Vocabulary Ideas

- Sections that include the following:
  - quizzes
  - hands-on projects
  - cooperative-learning activities
  - cross-curriculum connections

- Post-reading Activities

- Research Ideas

- Culminating Activities

- End-of-Unit Assessments

- Answer Key

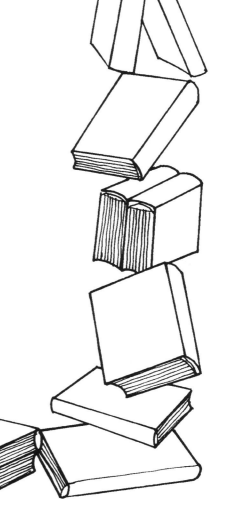

Sample Lesson Plans

Each of the lessons may take from one to several days to complete. Teachers should feel free to modify the plans to meet their teaching styles and the specific needs of their classes.

Lesson 1
- Introduce and complete selected pre-reading activities. (page 5)
- Read "About the Author" with your students. (page 6)
- Introduce the vocabulary list for Section 1. (page 9)

Lesson 2
- Select a vocabulary activity to complete before reading. (page 10)
- Read chapters 1–8. Review vocabulary within the context of the story as you read.
- Research and complete the map of Missouri. (page 15)
- Read about the Mississippi River and its riverboats. (page 16)
- Create a model of an 1800s town for reference as you read the rest of the book. (page 12)
- Add costumed people to the town model or create costumed dolls. (page 13)
- Complete the Southern Dialect handout. (page 14)
- Administer the Section 1 quiz. (page 11)
- Introduce the vocabulary list for Section 2. (page 9)

Lesson 3
- Select a vocabulary activity to complete before reading. (page 10)
- Read chapters 9–15. Review vocabulary within the context of the story as you read.
- Read and complete handout on the roles of women in Twain's Life. (page 18)
- Discuss "Changing Roles for Men and Women." (page 20)
- Discuss other changes that have occurred since the 1800s, like popular home remedies. (page 19)
- Administer the Section 2 quiz. (page 17)
- Introduce the vocabulary list for Section 3. (page 9)

Lesson 4
- Select a vocabulary activity to review before reading. (page 10)
- Read chapters 16–22. Review vocabulary within the context of the story as you read.
- Read about pirates and assign appropriate activities. (pages 22–23)

- Complete "Use Your Senses" worksheet. (page 24)
- Administer the Section 3 quiz. (page 21)
- Introduce the vocabulary list for Section 4. (page 9)

Lesson 5
- Select a vocabulary activity to complete before reading. (page 10)
- Read chapters 23–30. Review vocabulary within the context of the story as you read.
- Assign "Staging the Scene" and "Creating a Courtroom." (pages 26–27)
- Create a historical newspaper. (page 28)
- Make copies of the newspaper to distribute during the culminating activity.
- Administer the Section 4 quiz. (page 25)
- Introduce the vocabulary list for Section 5. (page 9)

Lesson 6
- Select a vocabulary activity to complete before reading. (page 10)
- Read chapters 31–36.
- Complete and discuss "Cave Exploration." (page 30–31)
- Complete and discuss "Money, Maps, and Measurements." (page 32)
- Read and complete "Your Financial Future." (page 33)
- Administer the Section 5 quiz. (page 29)

Lesson 7
- Discuss any questions your students may have about the story. (page 34)
- Assign book reports and research projects. (pages 35–36)
- Begin work on culminating activities. (pages 37–41)

Lesson 8
- Choose and administer assessment(s). (pages 42–44)
- Discuss test answers and possibilities.
- Discuss the students' enjoyment of the book.
- Provide a list of related reading for your students. (page 7)

Pre-reading Activities

Imagine taking a family on vacation with no money, no map, and no fuel in the car. Before someone goes on a trip, he or she generally spends time preparing in order to have an enjoyable journey. For students to have a good journey on their reading adventures, they also need some preparation. Here are some ideas to do just that before they begin reading *The Adventures of Tom Sawyer*.

1. Hannibal is the dusty little town on the Mississippi River where Twain spent his boyhood and is the place upon which he based the setting of *Tom Sawyer*. Ask students to investigate facts about Hannibal, Missouri, and have them design travel brochures.

2. Using reference materials from the library or Internet, draw or trace a carriage from the 1800s onto a large cardboard box. Cut ovals in the places where the faces would be of the people sitting in the carriage. Let students pose behind the cardboard. Take pictures with an instant or digital camera and post these pictures in the hall, library, or on the bulletin board. You may also want to use a picture to put in the local or school paper. Keep the carriage for use in Southern Day activities (see page 37).

3. Arrange students into groups and ask them to brainstorm a list of all the things they believe did not exist in the 1800s. Students can refer to the list as they read the story or conduct research to see if they were correct.

4. Look up Mark Twain's famous sayings in *Bartlett's* or another resource. Have students select their favorites, write them on sentence strips, and post them around the room. Alternately, ask students to write a paragraph or two about why a quote has particular meaning or humor for them.

5. Students can use the Internet to visit the Web site *www.classiclit.about.com* to search for online copies of Mark Twain's autobiography as well as Susy Twain's biography of her father. Students can read a chapter from each work, then write about and/or discuss the differences between the two perspectives.

6. Take students to a public library where, using microfiche, they can research old newspaper articles from the 1800s. Ask them to write down headlines of the day. Discuss what they think the world was like then as opposed to now.

7. Direct students to research pictures of steamboats and then to create models using craft sticks, paper, glue, and markers. Award prizes and then display the models in the library.

About the Author

Putting snakes in his mother's sewing basket, dropping watermelon rinds on his brother's head, and hiding bats in his pockets were not just the acts of Tom Sawyer—they were the real life antics of Tom's creator, Samuel Langhorne Clemens. Like Tom, Samuel was a boy who always seemed to be in trouble.

Samuel Langhorne Clemens was born on November 30, 1835, in Florida, Missouri. He grew up in the small Southern town of Hannibal, Missouri, located on the Mississippi River. Clemens spent much of his childhood playing on the banks of the great river and watching the steamboats travel upon it. At 12, he quit school to become an apprentice to his brother Orion. Later, he left his brother and worked as a newspaperman in both Philadelphia and New York.

Eventually, he returned to Missouri, where he fulfilled his childhood dream: working as an apprentice to a steamboat pilot. During this time, he began calling himself "Mark Twain," a river term which meant "safe water—twelve feet deep." He would stay on the river for only four years, however, before briefly fighting in the Confederate Army during the Civil War.

In 1865, Twain first had a story published, "Jim Smiley and His Jumping Frog" (a title which was later changed to "The Jumping Frog of Calveras County"). This success encouraged him to pursue becoming a full-time writer.

The unpaid editor of most of his works was his wife Olivia Langdon Clemens, whom he married in 1870. She read all of his manuscripts and marked the parts that she did not like. Together, Twain and his wife moved to Hartford, Connecticut; had four children; and built a 19-room house. After Twain began to publish and speak, he became a very wealthy man. However, he occasionally lost money due to poor investments. He was so popular, though, that all he needed to do to regain his wealth was to travel on another speaking tour.

Although Twain lead an exciting life, it ended in sadness when he died of heart disease at the age of 74, having outlived three of his children and his beloved wife.

References

Hornung, Clarence P. *The Way It Was in the USA: The South*. Abbeville Press, New York, NY, 1978.

McCutcheon, Marc. *Everyday Life in the 1800s*. Writer's Digest Books, Cincinnati, Ohio, 1993.

Reader's Digest Family Encyclopedia of American History. Pleasantville, NY.

Wilson, Charles Reagan and Ferris, William. *Encyclopedia of Southern Culture*. University of North Carolina Press, Chapel Hill, NC, 1989.

Chronological List of Works by Mark Twain

The following is a list of works by Mark Twain. Students may wish to read other works by the author.

1865. "The Celebrated Jumping Frog of Calaveras County"

1869. *Innocents Abroad, or The New Pilgrim's Progress*

1872. *Roughing It*

1873. *The Gilded Age* (with Charles Dudley Warner)

1876. "The Facts Concerning the Recent Carnival of Crime of Connecticut"

1880. *A Tramp Abroad*

1882. *The Prince and the Pauper*

1882. "The Stolen White Elephant"

1883. *Life on the Mississippi*

1884. *The Adventures of Huckleberry Finn*

1889. *A Connecticut Yankee in King Arthur's Court*

1891. "Luck"

1892. *The American Claimant*

1893. "The $1,000,000 Bank Note"

1894. *The Tragedy of Pudd'nhead Wilson and the Comedy of Those Extraordinary Twins*

1896. *Personal Recollections of Joan of Arc*

1896. *"Tom Sawyer Abroad," "Tom Sawyer, Detective," and Other Stories*

1897. *"How to Tell a Story" and Other Essays*

1899. "The Man that Corrupted Hadleyburg"

1902. "The Five Boons of Life"

1902. "Was It Heaven? Or Hell?"

1916. *The Mysterious Stranger*

Book Summary

By the third line of the novel, the main character of Mark Twain's book is already in trouble, and that is the way he remains for nearly the entire book. Tom Sawyer, an impish but charming boy, enjoys everything about growing up on the banks of the Mississippi except going to school and sitting still.

In the first chapter, Tom has escaped school, but Sid, his younger half-brother, turns him in to Aunt Polly, their guardian. As punishment, Tom must whitewash a fence. As usual, Tom manipulates the situation so that his friends paint the fence for him for the privilege of so doing.

Tom next turns his attention to impressing the new girl, Becky Thatcher. When his initial success sours, he roams after dark with the town orphan, Huck Finn. There, Tom and Huck witness the murder of young Dr. Robinson by Injun Joe, who then tries to frame the town drunk for the murder. Fearing for their lives, Tom and Huck take an oath never to tell anyone what they saw.

With so many difficulties, Tom decides to leave town with friends Huck Finn and Joe Harper, running away to a remote island. While the boys pretend to be pirates, the townspeople conclude that the boys have drowned. When the boys return home, they show up at their own funerals and become heroes.

Tom and Becky's relationship is mended, but they are separated when she leaves town for the summer. Tom also gets sick and, upon his recovery, decides to testify at the town drunk's trial. After Tom's testimony, Injun Joe escapes and Tom fears the killer's revenge.

With the trial over, Tom and Huck take off to a dilapidated old house to look for treasure. They find Injun Joe talking to an acquaintance about his own treasure, for which Tom and Huck decide to hunt. However, Becky sidetracks Tom, who joins her on a picnic while Huck continues searching. Tom and Becky then get lost in a cave where, it turns out, Injun Joe has been hiding. After Tom and Becky escape, the townspeople seal the cave, unknowingly trapping Injun Joe inside, where he dies of starvation. Huck and Tom finally reunite and figure out that Injun Joe's treasure is in the cave. The two boys become wealthy as a result of their find. Huck discovers, however, that wealth is not as valuable as freedom. We leave him at the end of the book considering giving up his money for the freedom of the riverbanks.

Vocabulary Lists

The vocabulary words listed below correspond to each section of *The Adventures of Tom Sawyer*. Creative ideas for presenting new vocabulary are on page 10.

Chapters 1–8

perplexed	alacrity	frivolity
sagacity	furtive	accouterments
derision	morosely	shorn
ambuscade	effusion	mortified
adamantine	adherent	fetters
melancholy	abash	facetious
tranquilly	ostentation	

Chapters 9–15

inarticulately	derision	apprehensive
stolid	formidable	valance
apprehensively	phrenological	succumb
plausibility	ventilation	rendezvous
andiron	consternation	conjectured
impudence	alloy	purloined
regalia	avariciously	

Chapters 16–22

mutinous	Elysian	vexation
stupendous	eloquent	onslaught
oppressiveness	irresolute	exultation
lethargy	lacerate	lethargy
soliloquized	pummeling	immense
persistently	ingenious	gesticulation
repentant	urchin	

Chapters 23–30

solitary	sepulchral	conspicuous
prosecution	solemnities	deposed
lavishly	auspices	cross-examined
infested	labyrinth	foreshadowed
formidable	verdict	defense
obliterated	sauntered	delirium
apprehensive	haggard	

Chapters 31–36

vagabond	somber	diverging
episode	laudations	fatigue
posse	lucid	moiety
embellishment	proprietor	oppressive
prodigious	frescoed	apathy
remoteness	bewitching	effusive
traversed	perilous	

Vocabulary Activity Ideas

After reading the vocabulary list, you know that Twain's language usage was colorful and will be, at times, an exciting challenge for students. Try some of the following ideas to introduce new vocabulary.

1. Play "Dictionary Race." Write new words on word cards or cut poster board into appropriately sized cards. Give each student a dictionary. Hold up one word at a time for students and let them race to find it in the dictionary. The first student to find the word needs to correctly state the page number on which he or she found it in order to earn a point. Then give every student time to find the correct page and to copy the definitions onto index cards or writing paper. Make sure everyone is finished before you continue on to the next word. The student with the most points at the end of the game wins.

2. Play "Context Clues." Group the students and then give them a work sheet with sentences that provide context clues for their vocabulary words. List four definitions for the vocabulary word below each sentence. Let students guess the correct definition. Students can correct their own work by taking turns looking up the word definitions. Each student who guesses correctly gets a point. The student (or students) with the most points at the end of the game wins.

3. Give students blank word search and crossword puzzle sheets. Students can create clues by writing definitions for the words needed to complete the puzzles.

4. Use index cards to play a matching game. Ask students to put their new words on one set of cards and definitions on another set. Ask students to spread the cards out facedown—word set on one side, definition on the other. Tell students the object of the game is to match the words with definitions. Each time students make a match, they keep the pair of cards. The students who have the most cards at the end of the game win.

5. Create pictorial dictionaries. Provide students with decorative covers. Ask them to write the words and definitions in their books and then either cut out or draw pictures to illustrate as many of the entries as possible.

Urchin   **Valance**

6. Play "Charades" with the new words. Divide the class into two teams. Have students take turns acting out definitions.

7. Group students and direct them to write short plays using the vocabulary words. Tape the plays and show them on a review day.

Quiz Time

1. Write a one-paragraph summary of the major events in chapters 1 through 8. Then complete the rest of the questions on this page.

2. Who is the author of *The Adventures of Tom Sawyer*? _____

3. Where is the story set? _____

4. How does Tom get caught for skipping school and going to the swimming hole? _____

   _____

   _____

5. How does Tom convince other boys to whitewash Aunt Polly's fence? How does his wealth increase during the day? _____

   _____

   _____

   _____

6. How does Tom act when he first notices the new girl, Becky Thatcher? What small gesture does she perform to encourage his attention? _____

   _____

   _____

7. What happens that hurts Tom's feelings? What scene does Tom imagine to comfort him?

   _____

   _____

   _____

8. How does Tom earn his Bible? _____

   _____

   _____

9. How does Tom's behavior in church create chaos during the sermon? _____

   _____

   _____

   _____

10. Would you have enjoyed living during Tom Sawyer's time? Why or why not? _____

    _____

    _____

    _____

Create an 1800s Town

Today, towns have cars whizzing up and down paved streets and planes flying overhead. That was not what life was like in Tom Sawyer's small town. Read the facts about life in the 1800s below. Then, using encyclopedias, textbooks, the Internet, and other reference materials, create a model of an 1800s town. Share your model with your classmates. (If you wish to include people in your town, you may want to refer to page 13, "Old-fashioned Fashions," for ways to clothe them.)

A variety of materials may be used for this project. Here are a few suggestions:

- Use construction paper, glue, and scissors to create a town in a shoebox.

- Use quick-drying modeling clay to create your town.

- Make your town out of stiff paper, with stand-up tabs on the backs of the buildings.

- Paint a town background on cardboard. Dress plastic dolls in period clothing and place them in your scene.

Facts About Towns in the 1800s

- At the beginning of the 1800s, nearly everyone worked on farms. Toward the middle of the century, many people left the farms in order to work in shops and in factories.

- The majority of doctors opened their practices without a degree. The common fee for a house call visit was one or two dollars.

- For socializing, most people attended church. Baseball began in 1823; football in 1870; and golf in the 1880s. Basketball was introduced in 1891; it was played with a soccer ball and two peach baskets. Bowling was played throughout the century. The circus began in 1830 when acrobatic troupes joined horse shows. Horse racing was popular throughout the century. Theater was performed in churches, tents, saloons, showboats, and concert halls.

- Travel was risky, at best. A coach with a team of horses was the most popular form of transportation. Cars came into existence in the late 1800s. In 1895, there were four cars in the entire country; but by 1900, there were 8,000 cars. The first transcontinental railroad in America was completed on May 10, 1869, joining the Central Pacific and Union Railroads in Promontory, Utah. Workers, mainly Chinese and Irish immigrants, slowly dynamited their way through the hardest granite, then moved all the rocks and laid the ties and rails by hand.

Old-Fashioned Fashions

The drawings below show examples of popular fashions in the middle 1800s and early 1900s.
Use them as models for townspeople (see page 12) or to make costumes for fashion dolls or simple
paper or cloth dolls. You may also make life-sized cardboard people dressed in the fashions of the day.
Cut ovals where the faces go and use the cardboard models to take souvenir portraits during
"Southern Day" (see page 37).

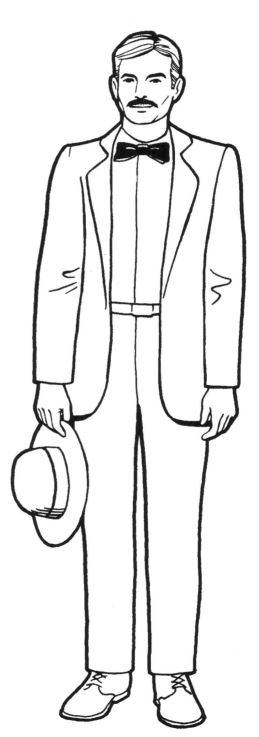

Southern Dialect

Over the years, two beliefs developed about Southern people's way of talking. Many believed that Southerners talked more slowly due to living in a hot climate. Others believed that the soft dialect resulted from the personality of the Southern people, who were reputed to be courteous and genteel; naturally, their language would be softer and slower.

Both of these beliefs, however, are only myths. The Southern speaking patterns developed because of the original people who settled there; the migration of other people into the area; and the topography of the region, which often isolated Southerners from the influences of other parts of the country.

In *The Adventures of Tom Sawyer*, Mark Twain's characters speak Southern dialect. One reason for this was that Twain was a master of Southern dialect and its many variations. When Twain went on speaking tours, he often entertained his audiences by reading or speaking in thick Southern dialects. Recently-discovered evidence shows that Twain worked and reworked the spellings of words in his written work to get the dialect just right. Today, however, readers sometimes find the dialects difficult to understand. To become acquainted with these speaking patterns before reading the novel, find a partner and try to read the sentences below aloud. Then try to translate the sentences into modern English. Your teacher will help you check your attempts.

1. "Tom, it was a middling warm in school, warn't it?" _____

   _____

2. "Oh, I dasn't, mars Tom. Ole missis she'd take an' tar de head off'n me. Deed she would."

   _____

   _____

3. "Well Sid don't torment a body the way you do. You'd be always into that sugar if I warn't watching you." _____

   _____

4. "I'm a-laying up sin and suffering for us both, I know. He's full of the Old Scratch, but laws-a-me! he's my own dead sister's boy, poor thing…" _____

   _____

5. "Can't, Mars Tom. Ole missis, she tole me I got to go an' git dis water an' not stop foolin roun' wid anybody." _____

   _____

Map of Missouri

Mark Twain and his fictional character Tom Sawyer both lived in the state of Missouri. Find a map of Missouri on the Internet or in an encyclopedia, atlas (either in book form or on a computer program), or other source. Locate the following places on the map below and label them. In addition to a compass rose, add a map key in which you identify a symbol for the state capital, cities, rivers, and mountains. When you are finished, on separate paper write five questions about the map for a classmate to answer.

Missouri River	**Poplar Bluff**	**Kansas City**	**Lake of the Ozarks**
Mississippi River	**Springfield**	**Independence**	**Ozark Plateau**
Jefferson City	**Hannibal**	**St. Joseph**	**Taum Sauk Mountain**
Columbia	**St. Louis**	**Joplin**	

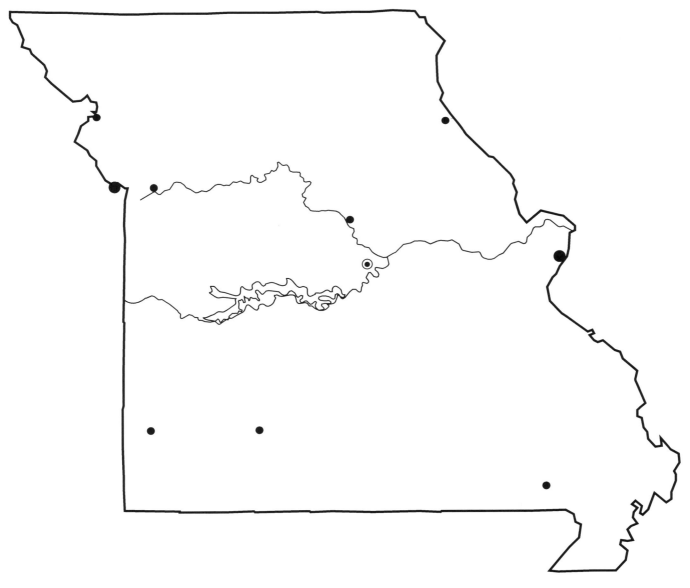

The Mississippi River

Tom Sawyer takes place in a small town on the banks of the Mississippi, where large steamboats carrying cargo and people regularly passed. Like other great rivers of the world, the existence of the Mississippi River has had great impact on the lives and communities of the United States. The Mississippi has been a tremendous economic and natural resource, as well as an inspiration for stories, poems, and paintings.

The Mississippi winds through the heart of the United States, passing by hundreds of communities, and millions of people from diverse cultures live along its shores. The river is known by several names, including the Father of Waters, Big Muddy, and Old Devil River.

Before the European settlers arrived, Native Americans used the river as an artery for travel, and they built religious structures called mounds along its banks. In 1673, a Jesuit missionary, Jacques Marquette, and an explorer, Louis Joliet, were the first Europeans to explore the Upper Mississippi River. The original river transportation was the canoe, and later keelboats that could be poled or pulled from shore were used because they could move more quickly. In 1811, the steamboat era began with the sailing of the *New Orleans*. The steamboat turned the nation's rivers into a system that could carry large amounts of cargo, as well as pioneers who would begin farms across the heartland.

Steamboat navigation on the Mississippi was risky, however. In fact, in river lingo, a sawyer is a fallen tree hidden under the surface of the river on which a boat could snag. The riverbanks widened with the clearing of forests for steamboat fuel and farmlands, causing the banks to erode and the river to shift. In his book *Life on the Mississippi*, Twain wrote that people "cannot tame that lawless stream, cannot curb or confine it, cannot say to it, Go here, or Go there, and make it obey . . . cannot bar its path with an obstruction that it will not tear down, dance over and laugh at."

Not until the 1930s was the Army Corps of Engineers able to successfully tame the river by building a series of 29 navigation dams that directed the flow of the Mississippi. The dams turned the river once more into an artery for commerce, power generation, and storm water collection.

Extension: If you had lived during the time of Tom Sawyer, you probably would have fished for your dinner. Using the library or the Internet, research species of fish that make their home in the Mississippi River. Illustrate the fish and create a mural by placing the fish, along with a label, on a background of blue butcher paper.

Quiz Time

1. When Tom can't sleep, where does he go? _____

2. What happens in the cemetery that Huck and Tom visit? _____

   _____

3. How do Huck and Tom react to what they see in the cemetery? _____

   _____

4. What is the oath that Huck and Tom take? _____

   _____

5. Why does Tom begin to have trouble sleeping? _____

   _____

6. Why does Becky stop coming to school? _____

7. List some of Aunt Polly's home remedies and tell what they are used to cure. _____

   _____

   _____

   _____

8. What events lead up to Tom running away? _____

   _____

   _____

9. What do the people of the town believe happened to the boys? _____

   _____

10. Why does Tom sneak back to town? _____

   _____

Real Women in Mark Twain's Life

The women who surrounded Mark Twain played important roles in his personal life as well as in his works. Read the following information about these women. After reading, answer the questions below.

Olivia Langdon Clemens

Olivia was Twain's beloved wife and the editor of most of his works. She died before her husband, which greatly saddened him. In fact, he proclaimed that he hated the human race after her death.

Jane Clemens

Jane was Samuel Clemens' mother. She was unpredictable, fun loving, and noted for her sense of humor.

Mary Fairbanks

A very influential non-family member, she and Twain met aboard the steamboat *Quaker City*. Twain viewed Fairbanks as a close friend, editor, and mother figure.

Susy Clemens

Susy was Twain's oldest daughter and his favorite. Twain listened carefully to her suggestions and ideas. She helped him take his work in a more serious direction. At the age of 23, she died from meningitis, devastating her father.

Jean Clemens

She was the youngest of the Twain children and an invalid. Like the other daughters, she listened to her father's works, but she and her father did not seem to bond as he had with his oldest daughter. Jean died in 1910.

Clara Clemens

Clara was the Twains' middle daughter. After her mother and elder sister had died, Clara was expected to become caretaker to both her father and her younger sister. Exhausted at age 35, she gave up that role. She married and moved to Europe, leaving her father and sister to take care of themselves. She later worked, however, to preserve Twain's image.

Questions

1. On which women do you believe the characters of Aunt Polly and Becky are based? Why?

2. Toward the end of his life, Mark Twain's writings became dark and angry. What life events related to these women may have influenced his somber writings?

3. Which woman do you think was most influential in encouraging Twain's sense of humor? Why?

Home Remedies

Aunt Polly knew a home remedy for nearly every ailment. Like most Americans in the early to mid 1800s, she probably needed to rely on her own medical expertise to heal common symptoms. In Aunt Polly's times, a town was fortunate to have a doctor—though the doctor may not have been much more knowledgeable about medicine than his patients. After the Civil War, there were many advances in medicine; but prior to then, medical knowledge was very limited. While many home remedies worked, some of them not only failed to cure anything, but actually caused symptoms to worsen.

Below are common home remedies of the Old South. After reading them, think about any home remedies that people still use today. Write these remedies on separate paper. For example, do you have a special cure for hiccups? Your teacher may want you to share these remedies with your class.

Baldness

If you were going bald in the Old South, your home remedy probably would not have helped your hair loss—but it would have helped you lose friends. One home remedy was to smear garlic on your head and only rinse it off once a week. If that did not work, you were advised to try a healthy glob of horseradish, vinegar, and egg yoke or raw onion juice on your head.

Headaches

If you had a headache, you could not go to the drugstore for aspirin. Instead, you had your choice of sipping on strong coffee or celery seed water, taking a walk, or applying a bandage soaked with turpentine and smeared with lard to your head. If you did not have a headache before the treatment, you probably had one after.

Bad Breath

If you were a man or woman with sour breath, you would have been advised to suck on rosemary ashes, rinse your mouth with lavender water, and brush your teeth with sage leaves.

Hair Control

Bad hair day? You could try combing sweet milk with rose perfume in it or castor oil with cologne—then hope the milk didn't sour in the heat or a wandering fly didn't get stuck in the oil.

Note: You can learn more about these remedies in *Home Remedies from the Old South* by Emily Thatcher (Tresco, 1975); ask your public librarian to locate a copy.

Changing Roles for Men and Women

You may have noticed that the characters in *Tom Sawyer* behave in traditional male and female roles. In fact, in the 1800s most women worked inside the home doing housework, cooking, and taking care of the children. Most men worked outside the home in their chosen professions. Today, men and women both have changing roles. Some fathers stay at home, cooking, cleaning, and taking care of the children. Some mothers choose to put their careers on hold and stay at home. Some parents work from home, using the computer. In many homes, both parents work outside the home. How and why did the roles of men and women change? For the answers to these questions, put the events listed below in order on the time line. Then, answer the thought-provoking questions below.

1971—Equal Rights Amendment to Constitution (introduced 1923 and passed 1972)
1964—Civil Rights Act of 1964 banned sexual discrimination in the work place
1848—Women's Rights' Movement launched at Seneca Falls, NY
1920—Women's Suffrage Amendment ratified
1960s—Women's Movement gains recognition

1800   1900

1901   2000

Questions

1. Do your parents or caretakers work inside or outside the home? _____

2. Do you believe your parents have traditional or nontraditional roles inside the home? Explain your answer. _____

    _____

    _____

3. What type of roles (traditional or nontraditional) do most of the characters in *Tom Sawyer* play? Explain your answer. _____

    _____

    _____

Quiz Time

1. How does Tom convince the boys to stay on the island? _____

   _____

2. When do the boys reappear in St. Petersburgh? _____

3. What does Tom tell Aunt Polly about his dreams? _____

   _____

   _____

4. Why does Tom decide he can be independent of Becky Thatcher? _____

   _____

5. How does Becky try to make Tom jealous? _____

   _____

6. What does Alfred Temple do to get revenge on Tom? _____

   _____

7. How does Aunt Polly find out Tom was telling the truth about kissing her on the cheek?

   _____

   _____

8. What does Becky do that almost gets her in trouble? _____

   _____

9. How does Tom save Becky from her punishment? _____

   _____

   _____

10. How do the younger boys get back at the schoolmaster during graduation?

    _____

    _____

    _____

Pirates

Tom and Huck enjoyed playing pirates, rogue robbers of innocent people on boats at sea. Pirates were a dangerous and real threat, however. Men would sign on board pirate ships under a captain, who would promise a reward—a percentage of captured gold, money, and other goods—for their work aboard the ship. Royalty, too, used pirates to help them increase their wealth. Queen Elizabeth, for example, commissioned Sir Francis Drake to pirate Spanish ships laden with gold and jewels.

Except for those moments when the pirates happened upon a victim, life at sea was dull. Bored pirates would fight among themselves, and, since they were lawless, the captain rarely intervened, allowing them to fight to the death. Pirates loaded up on bottled beer because they would be at sea for a long time without fresh water. They also ate hard tack (unappealing dry biscuits) and limes to fight scurvy.

The classic symbol on a ship's pirate flag is a skull and crossbones. A pirate ship captain also used this symbol to indicate a sailor's death in the ship's log. If a pirate ship flew a red flag, it symbolized that the sailors on board would show no mercy to their captives. The pirate flag is also known as a *jolly roger*, a term which probably comes from the French term *jolie rouge*, meaning *pretty red*. Either way, the sight of the pirates' flags struck fear in sailors and captains aboard other ships.

Here is some pirate vocabulary that Tom and Huck may have used.

- ✗ **booty**—stolen goods

- ✗ **bucaneer**—a pirate adventurer of the sea

- ✗ **cutlass**—short, single-edged sword favored by pirates

- ✗ **galleon**—a large, square-masted vessel of the 1500s used for war or commerce

- ✗ **jolly roger**—pirate flag

- ✗ **loot**—stolen gold, money, or other goods

- ✗ **maroon**—to isolate someone without resources

- ✗ **merchant ship**—a ship involved in commerce (e.g., a cargo ship)

- ✗ **mutiny**—to rise against naval or military authority

- ✗ **plunder**—the act of robbing

Pirates *(cont.)*

Complete one of the following activities to learn more about pirates.

- Investigate one of the well-known pirates listed below and make a "Most Wanted Criminal" poster for his or her capture.

    ✘ Anne Bonny

    ✘ Edward Teach (Blackbeard)

    ✘ Henry Morgan

    ✘ Jean Laffite

    ✘ Samuel Ballamy

    ✘ Sir Francis Drake

    ✘ William Kidd

- Create an illustrated pirate dictionary. Use the terms on page 22 and add additional sayings that you find, such as "Shiver me timbers."

- Research the types of ships used by pirates. Write an illustrated report.

- Investigate pirates from ancient times to the present. What items do pirates seek in today's world?

- Investigate pirate costumes. Write an illustrated report. Create costumed figures for display.

- Find out about pirates hired by royalty to capture treasure, such as Sir Francis Drake.

- Learn about treasure hunting. Compare the equipment treasure hunters use today with that used by pirates.

- Research pirate treasure. What type of coins or other loot might pirates have found aboard ships in the 1800s?

- Watch a movie such as *Peter Pan*, which features the infamous Captain Hook, or read a pirate book such as *Treasure Island*. Write your impressions about pirates.

- Enter the following key words into an Internet search engine to find Web sites about pirates:

    ✘ *famous pirates*

    ✘ *history*

    (**Note to instructor:** To ensure Internet safety, you may wish to preview the sites and bookmark them for students.)

- Write a scene about what may have happened had real pirates confronted Tom and Huck. Share the scene with the class through a role play.

Use Your Senses

Mark Twain's writing affects all of the reader's senses. Through Twain's descriptions, the reader is guided to see, smell, hear, taste, and feel life in a small town in Missouri. This ability to create sensory impressions is one of the reasons *The Adventures of Tom Sawyer* has become a classic piece of literature that is still read today.

Scan the book and write some things that Tom would see, hear, smell, touch, and taste in his world. Then think about and write a contrasting item that you would see, hear, smell, touch or taste in your own contemporary world.

Page Number	What did Tom and others sense then?	What do you sense now?
Example: *84*	*health periodicals and phrenological frauds*	*medical journals and prescription drugs*

Quiz Time

1. Why do you think Tom decides to testify? _____

   _____

2. What happens to Injun Joe during the trail? _____

   _____

3. What do Huck and Tom say they want if they find the treasure? What would you want if you discovered buried treasure? _____

   _____

   _____

4. Whom do they discover in the haunted house? _____

5. How do the boys escape from the house? _____

   _____

6. Where do Tom and Huck believe "number 2" is? _____

   _____

7. What big event do the Thatchers plan? _____

8. Describe McDougal's Cave. _____

   _____

   _____

9. What does Injun Joe plan to do to the Widow Douglas and why? _____

   _____

10. What does Huck decide to do to help the Widow Douglas? _____

    _____

Staging the Scene

Bring *Tom Sawyer* to life by staging the courtroom scene you read in Chapter 23. Working in small groups, rewrite the scene in play form. You may add characters or action to the scene, but do not change the plot. Use the diagram on page 28 to set up the classroom as a courtroom. When the groups have finished, each group reads its scene to the class. Select the best scene to act and videotape, then show it on "Southern Day" (page 37).

Before writing the scenes, discuss the meanings of the following legal terms in class:

Defendant: person accused of committing the crime

Defense attorney: lawyer who argues the case of the defendant

Prosecuting attorney: lawyer who argues the case of the people

Legal secretary: secretary to a lawyer

Court clerk: officer of the court who keeps records of trials and court proceedings

Bailiff: officer of the court in charge of keeping order, custody of the jury, and custody of any prisoners while court is in session

Judge: officer of the court who presides over the trial

Jury: group of citizens temporarily selected to listen to the facts of a case and decide whether the defendant is innocent or guilty

Witness: someone who testifies as to what she or he has seen or heard

Reminder: When writing a play, remember you are writing dialogue, or conversations between characters. If you want characters to perform an action, you need to write stage directions. Stage directions are written inside parentheses. Your teacher will review the format with you. Below is an example of dialogue to help you get started on your script.

Bailiff: It sure is a warm day, Marjorie.

Clerk: (*Marjorie sits down at her desk.*) Surely is Hank. I don't think it will get any cooler with all those people coming in here for the trial. (*Marjorie leans over and picks up a legal pad.*) I can't help but feel sorry for Muff Potter.

Creating a Courtroom

You can easily turn your classroom into a courtroom. Divide the students into groups and let them set up each section of the courtroom as shown below. Then stage the courtroom scene from *The Adventures of Tom Sawyer* (see page 26).

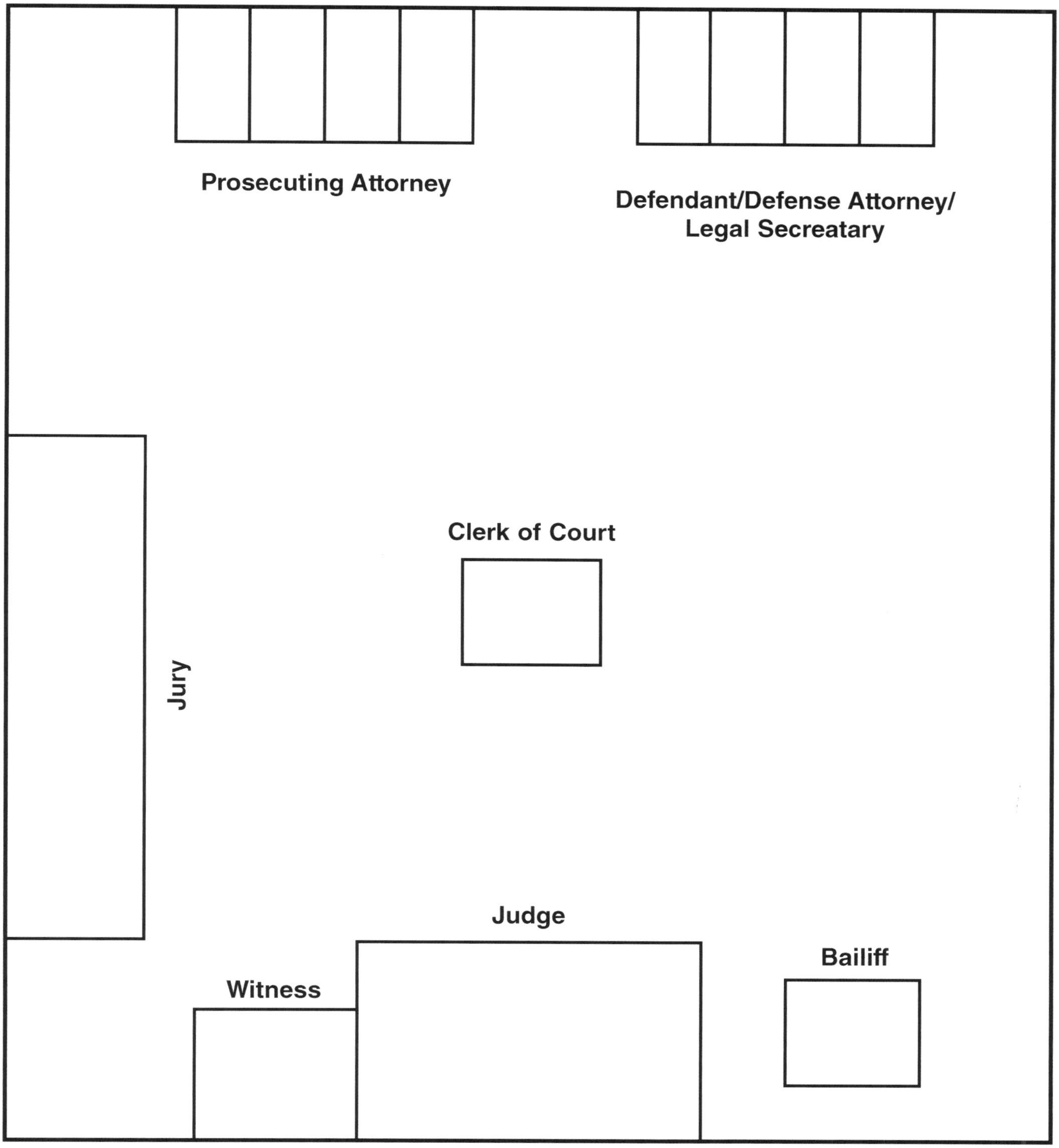

Prosecuting Attorney

Defendant/Defense Attorney/ Legal Secreatary

Jury

Clerk of Court

Judge

Witness

Bailiff

Historical Newspaper

The nineteenth century was an exciting time in which to be alive. Below are some of the major events that occurred during Mark Twain's lifetime. Select one of these events to investigate and then write a newspaper-like article reporting about the topic. Be sure to answer the questions who, what, when, where, and why. After everyone has completed this task, work together to create a historical newspaper. Your class may want to use the information obtained to create the following newspaper sections.

Current Events	**Business News**	**Advertisements**
Human Interest	**Editorials**	**Arts and Entertainment**

1835—Trail of Tears created by Apaches who were forced off their land

1845—Texas became a state

1850—California became a state; Missouri Compromise enacted

1859—Oregon became a state

1860—Abraham Lincoln elected president

1863—Civil War began on April 12 at Fort Sumter

1865—Civil War ended; Lee surrendered to Grant at Appomattox Court House, Virginia, on April 9

1868—Fourteenth Amendment passed, ending slavery

1869—Ulysses S. Grant elected president; first transcontinental railroad completed

1870—Fifteenth Amendment passed, permitting former slaves to vote

1876—Alexander Graham Bell invented the telephone

1877—Reconstruction of the South ended

1878—Thomas Edison invented the phonograph

1879—Thomas Edison invented the light bulb

1882—Jan Metzeliger invented a shoe-making machine

1896—Henry Ford used an assembly line to produce cars; *Plessy v. Ferguson* decision by Supreme Court permitted segregation by race

1898—Marie Curie discovered radium

Quiz Time

1. Whom does Huck recruit to help the Widow Douglas? _____

   _____

2. What happens to Tom and Becky during the picnic? _____

   _____

3. What happens to Huck while Tom and Becky are gone? _____

   _____

4. What survival skills does Tom use in the cave? _____

   _____

   _____

5. Whom does Tom discover in the cave? _____

   _____

6. How do Tom and Becky escape from the cave? _____

   _____

7. What happens to Injun Joe? _____

   _____

8. Why does Tom feel sorry for Injun Joe? _____

   _____

   _____

9. Where do Tom and Huck find the treasure? _____

   _____

10. Why does Huck leave the Widow's house? If you were Huck, would you have returned to the
    Widow's house? _____

    _____

    _____

Cave Exploration

Missouri is known for its many caves. In fact, to date people have discovered over 5,000 caves there. In the novel, Tom and Becky are lost in a cave for days before finding their way out. A few animals and cave formations they may have seen during their stay are shown below and on page 31. After looking at the animals and reading about cave formations, imagine that you explore an actual cave. Draw a picture of what you might see during your cave exploration.

Common Cave Animals

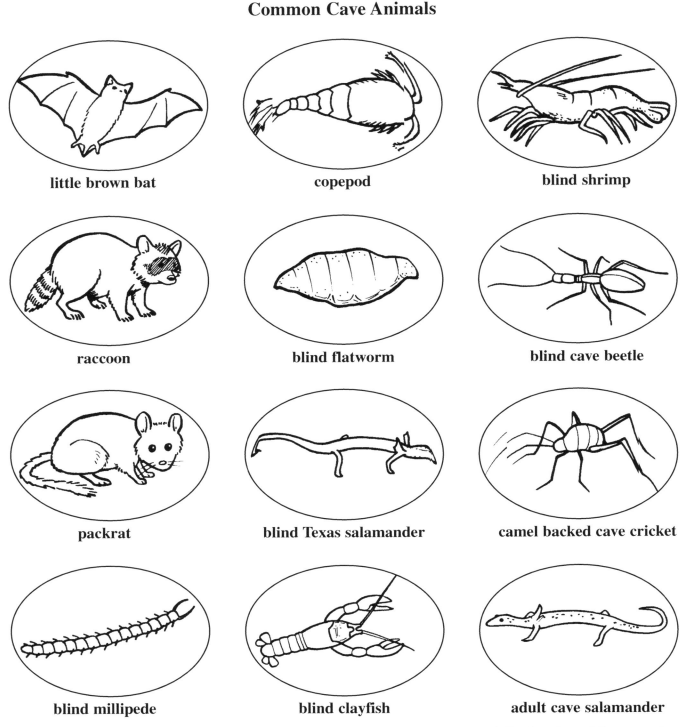

little brown bat   copepod   blind shrimp

raccoon   blind flatworm   blind cave beetle

packrat   blind Texas salamander   camel backed cave cricket

blind millipede   blind clayfish   adult cave salamander

Cave Exploration *(cont.)*

Common Cave Structures

Soda straws—These structures are thin, hollow tubes of calcite about ⊠" in diameter. Soda straws form when calcite-laden water runs through their centers, depositing rings of the mineral at the ends.

Stalactites—When the tips of the hollow tubes of soda straws clog, water flows outside of the soda straws and deposits mineral layers that form stalactites. Stalactites form from the ceiling down and often have pointed tips.

Stalagmites—Stalagmites are the opposite of stalactites because they grow up from the floor instead of down from the ceiling. Stalagmites form when mineral water drips from above the cave floor. Their tops are often flat or rounded.

Columns—When stalagmites and stalactites grow from the ceiling to the floor or when they connect to one another, they form columns.

Cave coral or popcorn—These structures are clusters of crystalline calcium carbonate that build up on walls and other formations.

Draperies—When mineral water leaves deposits that swirl and curl like curtains down the side of the inclined ceilings of the caves, they form draperies.

Flowstone—Flowstone forms when mineral water flows over the walls, floors, and other formations, depositing a thin sheet of calcium carbonate.

Cave Formations

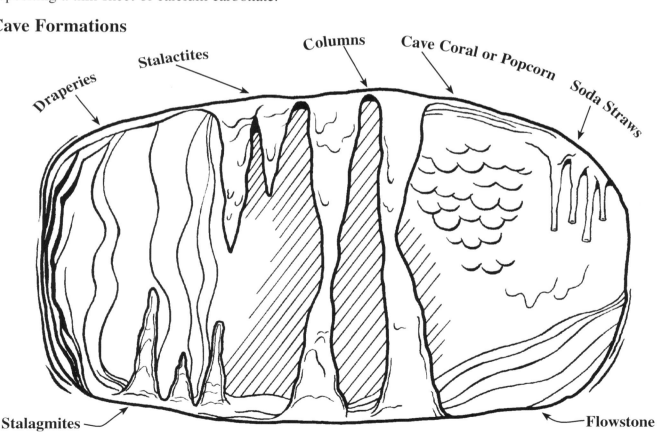

Bonus: What is another word for "cave explorer"?_____

Money, Maps, and Measurements

Try to figure out the riddles below by looking at the map. You will need a ruler for this activity.

1. Tom and Becky travel about 5 miles inside the cave. They turn right at the large rock and travel another ¾ mile. Where are they? _____

2. Tom searches for water. Give him directions from where he is now to the closest spot where he can find water. _____

3. Injun Joe is under the cross. Tom and Becky do not want to be anywhere near him. Where can they go so that they will be the farthest distance within the cave from Injun Joe? _____

   _____

4. Tom and Becky are at the large rock by the river. Help them escape by giving them directions to the crack in the top of the cave._____

5. Tom and Becky go back in the cave to find the treasure. How many miles must they travel to get to the cross from the cave opening? _____

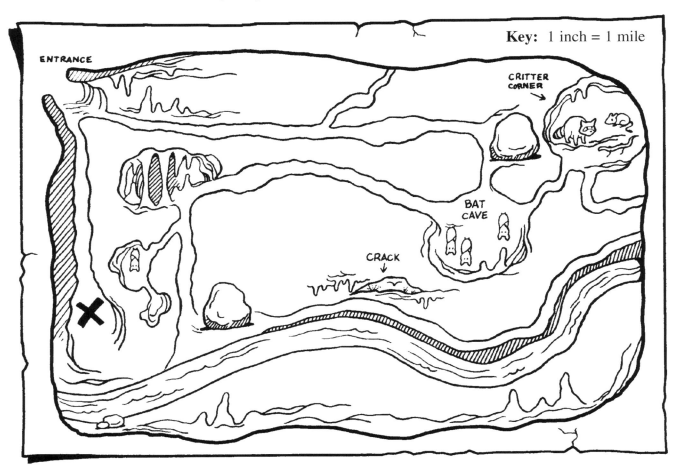

Your Financial Future

When Tom and Huck find Injun Joe's treasure, the adults in their lives invest the money so that the boys will never worry about their financial futures. Most people, however, do not have the luck to find hidden treasure or win the lottery. They must plan and save in order to buy the things they need or want and still have adequate funds set aside for retirement.

Have you ever thought about your own financial future? Read the statements below and check the one that best describes you:

_____a. I spend money as soon as I get it.

_____b. I save some of my money, and I spend some of my money.

_____c. I save all of my money until I get enough to buy something I really want.

_____d. I never spend any of my money.

According to financial advisors, you should spend some of your money, save some of your money, and give some of your money to charities. Work in small groups and discuss the following questions. Your teacher may ask groups to share their discussions with the class.

1. If you get an allowance, what, if anything, must you do each week in order to receive it?

2. Are there any expenses that you must cover with your allowance (e.g., brine shrimp for your fish or crickets for your lizard)?

3. Is giving any of your money to a charity important to you? Why or why not?

4. What would you want that you would like to be able to buy immediately? About how much does it cost?

5. How long would you have to save your allowance to buy one item on your list?

6. Is there anything you want that you would like to be able to afford in a year? in five years? About how much do these items cost? How much money would you need to save each week or month in order to be able to make this purchase?

Extension: With the help of adult family members, scan newspaper classifieds and other ads and create a realistic monthly budget for one person. Include savings, rent, utilities, food, car, gasoline, auto insurance, clothing, and entertainment. What is your monthly total? Are you surprised by the cost of living? Write a brief report about your findings and share it with the class.

Any Questions?

After you finished *The Adventures of Tom Sawyer*, did you have some questions that were left unanswered about the characters, setting, or plot of the story? Write them here.

_____

_____

_____

Next, working alone or in a small group, prepare possible answers for some or all of the unanswered questions you have asked. Then, working in the same way, answer the questions below to the best of your ability. When you have finished, share your ideas with the class.

- Do you think Huck and Tom remain as friends as they grow older? _____

- What happens to Tom and Becky's relationship? _____

  _____

- What type of person do you believe Sid becomes when he grows older?

  _____

- How do you think the Civil War affects Tom Sawyer's world? _____

  _____

- Do you think Tom and Huck choose careers or do they live on their wealth? What, specifically, do you think each one will do? _____

  _____

- Does Huck stay with the Widow or does he leave? _____

  _____

- Do you think Tom's wealth changes Aunt Polly's life? _____

  _____

- How do you think Sid and Tom's relationship changes as they grow older? _____

  _____

- How do you think the legend of Injun Joe changes as the years go by? _____

  _____

- Is Becky affected by the women's movement? If so, how? _____

  _____

  _____

Book Report Ideas

Allow students to choose from one of the following book report activities, or assign the one that you find most appropriate for your class.

Trivia Challenge

Students write questions about the book on the front and the answers on the back of index cards. As other students finish reading, let them play a trivia game as a review activity.

Moving Comic

Students make a moving comic theater using a shoebox with a window cut in it and a long sheet of white paper glued to two paper towel rolls. Students choose a scene to illustrate. Illustrations either can be captioned or the characters can have dialogue balloons above their heads.

Movie Script

Students write movie scripts based on a scene from the book. As with the actual movie *Tom Sawyer*, they may want to alter the scene to improve it cinematically. Students can produce the movies with willing volunteers from your class. After viewing, discuss the differences between the script and the book. Have the author discuss the changes he or she made and the reasons for the change.

Compare and Contrast

Students can compare and contrast the movie *Tom Sawyer* with the novel itself. What scenes from the book were left out from or added to the movie? How were the characters changed? How did the plot differ? What aspects of Tom were emphasized differently in the movie than in the book?

Quotation Poster

As students read, ask them to write quotations from the book that are meaningful to them. Then they can make and illustrate a poster with their quotations and display the posters around the room. Alternatively, to entice fellow students to read the books, display the posters outside your door or in the school or community library.

Challenging Vocabulary

After reading each chapter, students word process challenging vocabulary words onto their own disks. Then students word process the sentences in which the words occur in the book. After they have finished reading the book, students work together in a group to make a handout that contains these sentences as well as directions for their classmates to guess the vocabulary word meanings based on context. Classmates also should look up any words that have meanings they cannot guess by context.

Historical Connections

Decide in which time the novel was written. Prepare a report or a poster describing that time. Discuss how the novel is influenced by that period in history.

Research Ideas

The Adventures of Tom Sawyer was written during a historically exciting time that suggests many ideas for further research. You may select a topic from the list below or an original one that interests you. Be sure to check the topic with your instructor before you begin your project.

19th-Century America

Manners

Furniture

Role of Women

Architecture

Fashion

Education

Politics

Inventions

Science

Medicine

Transportation

Southern Culture

Food

Religion

Superstitions

Manners

Politics

Music

Myths of the South

Language

Women

Customs

Social Class

Civil War

General Topics

A soldier's daily life

Equipment of soldiers

Uniforms of the soldiers

Economics of the war

Slavery

Famous People of the Civil War

Robert E. Lee

Ulysses S. Grant

Abraham Lincoln

Nathan Bedford Forest

Stonewall Jackson

Jeb Steward

George McClellan

Jefferson Davis

Famous Battles

Gettysburg

Atlanta

Richmond

Natchez

Miscellaneous Topics

Dialects around the United States

Missouri

Hannibal, Missouri

Mark Twain and animals

Mark Twain overseas

Twain's many occupations

Important women in Mark Twain's life

Real people in Twain's novels

Pirates

Caves of Missouri

Southern Day

In a book as rich as *The Adventures of Tom Sawyer*, you can select many activities to use as culminating activities. One way to showcase all you've learned in one day and share it with others is to plan and participate in Southern Day. The easiest way to begin is to divide the students into groups and let each select different projects to work on. Below are suggestions for different groups. Write the names of each group member.

- Invitations

- Costumes

- Decorations

- Food

- Music

Group	Member

After the groups are selected, you may want to follow the basic checklist below. Write the date you completed the task.

1. Select a date.

2. Line up community and parent volunteers.

3. Send out a press release.

4. Send out invitations.

5. Monitor the groups as they work and help them set realistic deadlines for their projects.

6. Post a checklist for your students on the door of the classroom.

7. Make sure there is enough film and the batteries are charged on the camera.

8. Send out thank you notes after Southern Day.

9. Make sure there is a follow-up article in the newspaper.

10. Have the students make a scrapbook with pictures, newspaper clippings, and memorabilia.

Task	Date Completed

Invitation to Southern Day

Color the border and fill in the information on the invitation below. Then cut the invitation on the dotted line and present it to your family members.

Y'all Come Down Now, Y'Hear!

In honor of Mark Twain, Tom Sawyer, Huck Finn, Aunt Polly, and Becky Thatcher, we are celebrating great traditions of the South. Please come join us.

Date: _____

Time:_____

Place: _____

RSVP:_____

Southern Cooking

Southerners are famous for their hospitality. An important part of that hospitality is great food. Here are a few Southern dishes.

Crispy Fried Chicken

- 1½ to 2 pounds (675–900 g) chicken
- 1½ cups (350 g) flour
- salt and pepper to taste
- 2 beaten eggs
- 1 to 2 cups (225–450 g) crushed corn flakes
- oil (enough to cover the chicken)

Wash chicken and pat dry. Cut up chicken. Put flour in a bag with salt and pepper. Take one to two pieces of chicken at a time and roll in egg. If you want extra crispy chicken, roll the pieces in the corn flakes. Put pieces in bag with flour and shake until pieces are covered in flour. Shake off excess flour and put in the pan of oil. Cook chicken until brown and crispy.

Buttermilk Biscuits

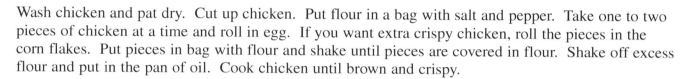

- 2½ cups (550 g) flour (after sifting)
- 1 cup (240 mL) buttermilk
- 1 teaspoon (5 mL) salt
- 2 tablespoons (30 mL) shortening
- ½ teaspoon (2.5 mL) baking soda

Preheat oven to 450° (230°C). Mix flour, salt, and soda and sift. Mix in shortening with tips of fingers, or chop with spoon. Add buttermilk, stirring with a spoon to make dough. Place dough onto a well-floured board, kneading it just long enough to get it smooth and firm enough to handle. Roll or pat out the dough to ½" thick. Cut with a floured biscuit cutter or glass. Place biscuits on a baking sheet and place in oven. Bake about 10 minutes, until golden.

Cream Gravy

After frying chicken, leave 2 to 3 tablespoons of oil and the browned crumbs in the pan. Add 2 tablespoons of butter and 4 tablespoons of flour. Blend and cook until golden brown. Add 1 cup of milk and 1 cup of hot water. Stir until smooth and the right thickness. Add salt and pepper to taste.

Southern Cooking *(cont.)*

Greens

- 1 to 2 bunches of turnip greens, collard greens, and/or mustard greens, rinsed well and trimmed

- ¼ pound (100 g) seasoning meat (e.g., ham)

Bring meat, water, and greens to a boil. Lower heat and cook slowly for 2 hours.

Sweet Iced Tea

- 3 large tea bags

- 1 cup (225 g) sugar

- 1 gallon (3.8 L) cold water

Put a few cups of water and three tea bags in a pan to boil. After water comes to a boil, take pan off burner. Let tea steep about 10 minutes. Pour into a container and mix with sugar. Stir until sugar dissolves. Pour remaining water into mixture and stir. Pour tea over glass filled with ice. Garnish with lemon and/or mint.

Southern Pecan Pralines

- 1 cup (225 g) white sugar

- 1 cup (225 g) brown sugar

- ½ cup (120 mL) evaporated milk

- ½ stick butter

- 1½ teaspoons (7.5 mL) vanilla

- 1 cup (225 g) pecan halves, toasted at 300° F for 5–7 minutes

- 1 pinch of baking soda

Butter a cookie sheet and set aside. Combine sugar and milk and stir over medium heat until it begins to boil. Add butter, pecans, and baking soda. Cook, stirring occasionally, until mixture reaches the soft-ball stage (this happens when you drop a bit of candy into cold water and it becomes a soft ball) or 240° on a candy thermometer. Take pan off heat and add vanilla. Beat mixture with a spoon until it looks cloudy and begins to get thick. Drop by teaspoonfuls onto the cookie sheet. Makes 12 large or 24 small pralines.

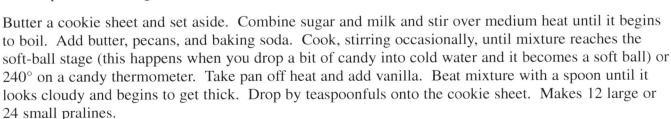

Southern Music

Music is a way for people to express their hopes, dreams, fears, and disappointments. Tom Sawyer certainly would have listened to music at church or an a picnic. Music has always been an important part of Southern culture and a major influence across the United States. Decide upon the type, or types, of Southern music you would like to feature at your Southern Day celebration. With your instructor's help, collect examples of the various kinds of music listed below so that your class can vote on what it would like to hear:

- Country
- Zydeco
- Cajun

- Bluegrass
- Gospel
- Western swing

You can add your own old-fashioned music fun by making some simple instruments in the classroom or at home. Some suggested materials for making music include the following:

- tin cans
- spoons
- wash tub drums with wooden spoon drumsticks
- cardboard roll, wax paper,
  and rubber bands to make kazoos;
  add beans and seal both ends to make maracas
- wash board or grater and spoon rasps
- trashcan lid cymbals
- comb and tissue paper harmonica

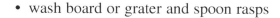

You may also be able to get access to percussion instruments such as tambourines, maracas, triangles, rasps, and cymbals. Practice playing with the music you have chosen before Southern Day. You may also have classmates (or family members) who are able to play Southern instruments such as the banjo; invite them to play their instruments as part of the celebration.

Objective and Essay Test

I. Matching

Match the descriptions of the characters to their names.

_____ 1. Huck Finn

_____ 2. Becky Thatcher

_____ 3. Judge Thatcher

_____ 4. Sid

_____ 5. Mary

_____ 6. Amy Lawrence

_____ 7. Injun Joe

_____ 8. Muff Potter

_____ 9. Peter

_____ 10. Mr. Dobbins

A. cat that teaches Aunt Polly

B. schoolmaster

C. seals McDougal Cave entrance

D. Tom's half brother

E. murderer of young Dr. Robinson

F. accused of the murder of Dr. Robinson

G. Tom's first girlfriend

H. new girl in town whom Tom likes

I. town orphan and friend to Tom Sawyer

J. acquired two Bibles at Sunday school for memorizing and reciting verse

II. True/False

Answer **T** for **True** or **F** for **False**

_____ 1. According to Mark Twain in the Prelude, most adventures recorded in the book never occurred in real life.

_____ 2. The story takes place in a small Southern town during the 1920s.

_____ 3. Aunt Polly genuinely loves Tom, although she has difficulty coping with him.

_____ 4. Injun Joe murders Dr. Robinson just for his money.

_____ 5. At the end of the book, Huck is glad he found the money because it gives him a chance to become civilized and to fit into society.

Objective and Essay Test *(cont.)*

III. Short Answer

Answer the questions in complete sentences.

1. Name two pranks that Tom pulls at the beginning of the story. _____

    _____

2. Describe your favorite adventure in the book. _____

    _____

3. Other than Tom, who do you believe is the most interesting character in the book? Explain.

    _____

    _____

4. Explain why you believe Tom's feelings change from fear to pity for Injun Joe.

    _____

    _____

IV. Essay

Tom Sawyer matures during the course of the book. Write a short essay, discussing ways in which Tom changes and events that you believe resulted in his gaining maturity.

_____

_____

_____

_____

_____

_____

_____

_____

_____

_____

Interpreting Quotations

On a separate sheet of paper, explain the meaning of the following quotations from *The Adventures of Tom Sawyer*.

Chapter 1

"He'll play hooky this evening, and I'll just be obleeged to make him work tomorrow to punish him. It's mighty hard to make him work Saturdays, when all the boys is having holiday, but he hates work more than he hates anything else, and I've GOT to do some of my duty by him, or I'll be the ruination of the child."

Chapter 2

"If he had been a great and wise philosopher, like the writer of this book, he would have comprehended that Work consists of whatever a body is obliged to do, and that Play consists of whatever is not obliged to do."

Chapter 4

"The boys were all eaten up with envy—but those that suffered the bitterest pangs were those who perceived too late that they themselves had contributed to this hated splendor by trading tickets to Tom for the wealth he had amassed in selling whitewashing privileges. These despised themselves, as being the dupes of a wily fraud, a guileful snake in the grass."

Chapter 12

"One of the reasons why Tom's mind had drifted away from its secret troubles was, that it had found a new bad weighty matter to interest itself about. Becky Thatcher had stopped coming to school."

Chapter 16

"But Joe's spirits had gone down almost beyond resurrection."

Chapter 22

"Now he found out a new thing—namely, that to promise not to do a thing is the surest way in the world to make a body want to go and do that very thing."

Chapter 25

"There comes a time in every rightly constructed boy's life when he has a raging desire to go somewhere and dig for hidden treasure."

Chapter 35

". . . withersoever he [Huck Finn] turned, the bars and shackles of civilization shut him in and bound him hand and foot."

Answer Key

Page 11

1. Answers will vary.

2. Samuel Clemens, known as Mark Twain

3. St. Petersburgh, a small southern town in the 1800s

4. Tom's half-brother Sid notices Tom's collar is sewn with black thread instead of white and he tells Aunt Polly.

5. Tom makes his friends believe that whitewashing is fun but will not let them have a turn, making them want one even more. Tom finally allows them to have a turn if they pay him with treasures. At the end of the day, Tom has collected such treasures as tin soldiers, pieces of orange peel, and firecrackers.

6. Tom stood in front of Becky's house showing off. Becky tossed a pansy over the fence before going inside.

7. Aunt Polly punishes Tom for breaking the sugar bowl when it was actually Sid's fault. He imagines Aunt Polly's grief and guilt if he (Tom) died.

8. Tom trades for enough tickets to get the Bible.

9. Tom becomes bored during the church service. He plays with a pinch beetle until it bites him; the beetle lands on the floor. A poodle wanders into the church, gets bitten by the bug, and wreaks havoc, disrupting the service.

10. Answers will vary.

Page 14

1. Tom, it was a little warm in school, wasn't it?

2. Oh, I better not, Master Tom. Old Mrs., she would tear my head off. Yes, she would.

3. Well, Sid doesn't cause problems like you do. You would always be into mischief if I weren't watching you.

4. I'm in enough trouble for both of us. He's full of the devil, but my goodness! He's my own sister's boy, poor thing . . ."

5. I can't, Master Tom. Old Mrs. told me to get the water without stopping to play with anyone.

Page 15

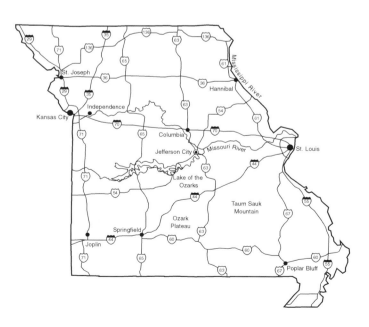

Answer Key *(cont.)*

Page 17

1. Tom goes to the cemetery with Huck Finn.

2. Tom and Huck witness the murder of young Dr. Robinson.

3. Tom and Huck are frightened.

4. Tom and Huck swear never to tell anyone about what they saw.

5. Tom was upset about the murder and felt guilty keeping Muff Potter's innocence a secret.

6. Becky is still ill.

7. Answers will vary.

8. Witnessing the murder; being unjustly accused of breaking the sugar bowl; having problems with his relationship with Becky

9. The townspeople believe Tom and Huck have drowned.

10. Tom is curious to know what the people in the town are saying about him.

Page 18

1. Answers will vary.

2. The death of Twain's wife and children

3. Answers will vary.

Page 20

1848—Women's Rights Movement launched at Seneca Falls, NY

1920—Women's Suffrage Amendment Ratified

1960—Women's Movement gains recognition

1964—Civil Rights Act of 1964 banned sexual discrimination in work place

1971—Equal Rights Amendment to Constitution

Page 21

1. Tom tells the boys about his plans to show up at their funerals the next day.

2. The boys reappear during their funerals.

3. Tom makes her believe that he dreamed the events of the night he actually sneaked into town. He also tells her that he kissed her in his dream.

4. The glory Tom received from his peers was enough. He didn't need Becky anymore.

5. Becky ignores him and talks to Alfred Temple.

Answer Key *(cont.)*

6. Alfred destroys Tom's spelling book, knowing that Tom will be the one to get punished.

7. Aunt Polly finds the piece of bark on which he writes, telling her they have gone pirating.

8. Becky accidentally tears the schoolmaster's book.

9. Tom says that he tore the book and takes the whipping.

10. The boys lower a cat on the schoolmaster's head during graduation. The cat grabs the wig off his head in front of everyone at the ceremony.

Page 25

1. Answers will vary.

2. After Tom testifies, Injun Joe jumps out the window of the courtroom and runs away.

3. Huck wants a piece of pie with a glass of soda everyday, and he wants to go to every circus that comes along. Tom wants a new drum, a real sword, a red necktie, a bull pup, and to get married. Students' answers will vary.

4. Injun Joe and the Spaniard are in the house.

5. Tom and Huck wait until the men eat and go to sleep, and they sneak out of the house.

6. Tom and Huck think that "number 2" is at one of Injun Joe's favorite hangouts, a tavern.

7. The Thatchers plan a town picnic.

8. McDougal's Cave is very large, "a vast labyrinth of crooked aisles that ran into each other and out again and led nowhere." The cave was so large and complex that no one in the town knew that cave well.

9. Injun Joe plans to take revenge on Widow Douglas because her deceased husband, a judge, had Injun Joe horsewhipped for vagrancy. Injun Joe plans to destroy the widow's appearance.

10. Huck runs to the nearby Welshmen and tells them the story.

Page 29

1. Huck gets help from the Welshmen.

2. Tom and Becky get lost in the cave.

3. Huck becomes ill and stays with the Widow Douglas.

4. Answers will vary.

5. Injun Joe

6. Tom finds a crack in the cave. He and Becky escape through the opening.

7. Judge Thatcher seals the cave. Injun Joe is in the cave and dies of starvation.

Answer Key *(cont.)*

8. During his time in the cave, Tom was hungry, too. He empathizes with the pain Injun Joe must have suffered.

9. Tom and Huck find the treasure in the cave.

10. Huck longs for his freedom. He hates having to be "civilized." Student answers will vary.

Page 31

Spelunker is another word for "cave explorer."

Page 32

1. Bat Cave

2. Travel about three miles down the path. Make a left turn. Travel about two miles to the river.

3. Critter Corner

4. Travel one and a half miles down the river to the crack in the cave.

5. About two and a half miles.

Page 42

I. 1. I   6. G

   2. H   7. E

   3. C   8. F

   4. D   9. A

   5. J   10. B

II. 1. F

   2. F

   3. T

   4. F

   5. F

III. Answers will vary.

Made in the USA
Monee, IL
07 January 2020